SOCIAL SURVIVAL

Social Survival is a practical manual outlining what it means to be a logical thinker and how logical thinkers can make sense of the social world. Relevant for young logical thinkers including those with high-functioning autism and Asperger's syndrome, this book clearly outlines how social confusion might arise and how this can be overcome.

Written in a clear and unpatronising style, the book considers a range of different social scenarios and breaks these down into manageable components with helpful activities to be completed by the young person. Chapters discuss the nature and benefits of logical thinking, nuances of language and communication in social situations, and the intricacies of social etiquette and peer interaction.

Features include:

- appealing visual resources;
- practical activities around social situations that are relevant to young people;
- blank templates which can be photocopied and are available for download online;
- guidance for family members on how to encourage ongoing communication;
- an action plan which can be personalised for different scenarios.

Social Survival will be essential reading for health, social care and education professionals and parents working with those who have high functioning autism or Asperger's syndrome or those who are logical thinkers who do not have a diagnosis. In addition, this book can be used independently by the young person themselves.

Amy Eleftheriades has 20 years' experience working with children and young people in a range of settings as a Residential Social Worker, teacher, SENCO and as an Advisor to schools. She now provides training to schools and families to support better communication for children with Autism Spectrum Disorders through her own organisation, Alpha Inclusion.

SOCIAL SURVIVAL

A Manual for those with Autism and Other Logical Thinkers

Amy Eleftheriades

Routledge
Taylor & Francis Group

LONDON AND NEW YORK

First published 2018
by Routledge
2 Park Square, Milton Park, Abingdon, Oxon OX14 4RN

and by Routledge
711 Third Avenue, New York, NY 10017

Routledge is an imprint of the Taylor & Francis Group, an informa business

British Library Cataloguing-in-Publication Data
A catalogue record for this book is available from the British Library

Library of Congress Cataloging-in-Publication Data
Names: Eleftheriades, Amy, author.
Title: Social survival : a manual for those with autism and other logical
    thinkers / Amy Eleftheriades.
Description: New York : Routledge, [2018] | Includes bibliographical
    references.
Identifiers: LCCN 2017058564 (print) | LCCN 2018017282 (ebook) | ISBN
    9781315142081 (ebook) | ISBN 9781138306899 (pbk.)
Subjects: LCSH: Autistic children—Behavior modification. | Social
    interaction in children. | Social skills in children.
Classification: LCC RJ506.A9 (ebook) | LCC RJ506.A9 E44 2018 (print) | DDC
    618.92/85882—dc23
LC record available at https://lccn.loc.gov/2017058564_

ISBN: 978-1-138-30689-9 (pbk)
ISBN: 978-1-315-14208-1 (ebk)

Typeset in Helvetica
by Apex CoVantage, LLC

Visit the eResources: www.routledge.com/9781138306899

Contents

Acknowledgements

As always, there have been a number of people who have inspired, encouraged and supported this book.

Firstly, thank you to Professor Howard Gardner and Professor Simon-Baron Cohen for their inspiring work and also for letting me use their ideas to help explain our differences. Also to Ian Gilbert for his thought-provoking 'Thunks®'.

Secondly, a heartfelt thank you to all of the young people and their families who continue to teach me. A special 'thank you' to Alvin, whose logical mind was extremely helpful during proofreading!

To my family and friends who have endured many discussions on processes, viewpoints and the amusing nature of the English language. Thank you.

Finally, special thanks must go to Teague who continues to support me and Sophia who has just started on her journey of World exploration.

How to use this book

Chapter 1 introduces you to the idea of being a logical thinker and gives you some information from some intelligent people about the different ways we process the world around us. It also contains some activities to help you think about yourself and others.

Chapters 2 and 3 contain guidelines on different areas of social communication and interaction. They are not set rules (unfortunately there are only a few set rules for these types of experiences). Each chapter contains some activities to complete alone or with your Social Interpreters (see below).

Social Interpreters

These are people who can help you navigate your way around the book and life in general, if needed. They are people who are already in your life. There is a section explaining about their role and helping you identify them and there are opportunities throughout the book for you to work together.

Activities

Throughout the book there are diagrams, tables and charts for you to use to practise skills. There are not many clear 'right' and 'wrong' rules when it comes to social communication and interaction and it is important that you try things out with the people around you in the context you are in.

Use the activities at times that suit you and feel free to adapt diagrams and tables if necessary.

You do not have to complete the activities in any particular order.

At the back of each chapter there are pages for you to make notes, jot down ideas and draw out your thoughts if needed.

Chapter 4 – Action plan is designed to help you examine what is important for you and identify the skills you need to get there. It may be useful to help you plan which skills you are going to prioritise.

Only use the action plan if it suits you.

This is your book. Adapt if necessary and develop all the ideas so they are true for the context you find yourself in.

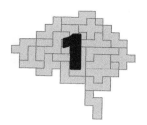

BEING A LOGICAL THINKER

Understanding yourself

Do you tend to work things out logically? Are you systematic in the way you approach tasks and solve problems? Ever wondered why some people don't seem to understand what you mean and others just don't make any sense at all? Do others tell you to make the 'right choice' without being clear what they perceive the 'right choice' to be? Do you ever wonder if there is something different about you, or them?

It may well be that you simply are a logical thinker, and see the world in a different way to others. This book is about considering about whether you observe, analyse and engage in tasks, conversations and relationships in a logical way and it attempts to offer an explanation of different ways of thinking as well as some practical tools to help you negotiate the minefield of social interaction and communication.

Let's start with the admission that we are human, and so this book, as it has been written by a human, is not necessarily factual, and in fact, there may be many aspects you do not think are like you and other things that you can relate with.

This is OK.

Being human means we are complex.

We have our own thoughts, feelings and ideas and have experienced life in different ways to others. As much we might wish we could predict others' behaviour and that their actions always made sense; beings which can be programmed to produce predictable results, the human element means this is not always possible.

This is not a book about how to change yourself or please other people. It is a book to further your understanding, generate questions and develop ideas on social communication and interaction.

This book offers guidelines and information about some areas of social communication and interaction that may interest you. The activities are there for you to try out and see if they give you better understanding of human behaviour. If you are happier or more OK in social situations afterwards, this is great.

It does not mean you should change who you are, although developing ourselves and learning new ways to behave could be a good thing.

It is extremely important that you learn to be happy with who you are as a person. The way you think is important and what you do and how you do it is important too. This book may help you find ways to relate and communicate with others, if that is what you want.

Types of thinker

Professor Simon Baron-Cohen has done research on how we think and behave as people and he has written books and research papers over many years. Here is one of the ways he believes we can think about differences:

There are different ways that we process information and understand the world.

Empathizing

'**Empathizing is the drive to identify another person's emotions and thoughts, and to respond to them with an appropriate emotion**' (Baron-Cohen, 2004, p.2).

It is the ability to understand and relate to other people's feelings, thoughts and attitudes. People who are highly empathic will be able to understand why others behave in particular ways and can instinctively feel what another person may be feeling.

They may be able to predict how someone may react in particular circumstances.

So, a highly empathic person may be able to feel that someone is upset when their pet dies and responds by offering words of comfort.

Systemizing

'**Systemizing is the drive to analyze, explore, and construct a system. The systemizer intuitively figures out how things work, or extracts the underlying rules that govern the behavior of a system. This is done in order to understand and predict the system, or to invent a new one**' (Baron-Cohen, 2004, p.3).

People who are good systemizers can instinctively recognize and interpret systems and are able to identify and apply rules.

Once rules are understood, a good systemizer can use them to predict things that will occur in that system.

So, for example someone who is a systematic thinker may be able to use the calendar system to predict which day of the week 24th January will be on in 20 years' time.

Professor Simon Baron-Cohen writes about how some people tend to be better at empathizing and others are more systematic in their approach to the world. He does not say one way is better than the other, just that there are differences.

Let's use these ideas and put them on scales where 10 = extremely good and 0 = not good at all:

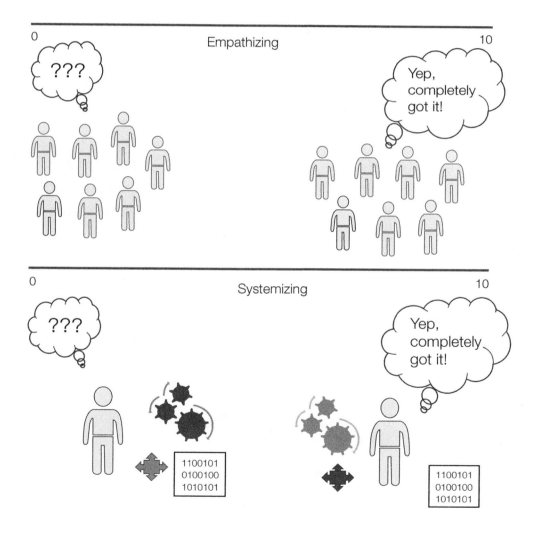

So if everyone put themselves on the scales, we would see some are better at systemizing, some are better at empathizing while others may be particularly good at both.

This means that some of us relate more to the empathic way of thinking and processing, and respond to people and situations better whilst others apply more logic to the world as we see it.

Intelligently different

Professor Howard Gardner is someone else who has researched people and how we work. He doesn't see intelligence as a single scale, or number but as types. So, it is not 'How intelligent are you?' that we should ask, but 'In what ways are you intelligent?'

Gardner believes we are all intelligent in different ways and that one way is not superior or inferior to the others. Each way of being intelligent represents how we process information. Below are some of the ways he thinks we are intelligent.

Linguistic intelligence

An ability to analyze information and create products involving oral and written language such as speeches, books, and memos.

Logical-mathematical intelligence

An ability to develop equations and proofs, make calculations, and solve abstract problems.

$$(m \times c) = h^2 + 3$$

Spatial intelligence

An ability to recognize and manipulate large-scale and fine-grained spatial images.

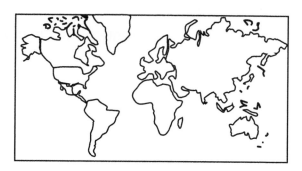

Musical intelligence

An ability to produce, remember, and make meaning of different patterns of sound.

Naturalist intelligence

An ability to identify and distinguish among different types of plants, animals, and weather formations that are found in the natural world.

Bodily-kinaesthetic intelligence

An ability to use one's own body to create products or solve problems.

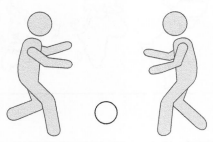

Interpersonal intelligence

An ability to recognize and understand other people's moods, desires, motivations, and intentions.

Intrapersonal intelligence

An ability to recognize and understand his or her own moods, desires, motivations, and intentions.

Professor Howard Gardner believes we can improve on any of these areas, but we may find we are naturally better in some areas more than others. With practice, we may be able to improve on all areas.

You can read much more about Professor Simon Baron-Cohen's and Professor Howard Gardner's ideas in their books and research papers.

So, how does this relate to you?

Well, think about yourself.

Do you have a better understanding of analytical puzzles than of why people around you behave in the way they do?

Do processes and systems interest you more than sitting around chatting about people?

Do you 'just know' about systems and processes in the areas that are of interest to you and maybe find it difficult how to explain to others how you 'just know'?

If we process information and understand the world around us in different ways, it makes sense that we will feel more comfortable completing particular tasks.

Others may appear to be better at other things and instinctively 'just know' how to do complete different activities and tasks.

You may want to complete the two activities below on 'The Scales of Thinking' and 'How Are We Intelligent?'

You may also want to complete different questionnaires devised by Baron-Cohen and Gardner which will give you more information about how you process information (see the back of the book for references on where you can find these).

The scales of thinking

0	Empathizing	10

0	Systemizing	10

The higher up the 'Empathizing' scale someone is, the more they understand others' thoughts, feelings and behaviour. They may use this way of processing to make sense of the world and to respond to situations.

The higher up the 'Systemizing' scale someone is, the more they are able to complete analytical puzzles, systematically work through problems and understand patterns. They may use this way of processing to make sense of the world and respond to situations.

Where would you put yourself on these scales?

Where would you put your family members?

Where would you put people from school, clubs (sports or social clubs, not the weapon!) or work?

Where would you put some famous people?

How are we intelligent?

Think about the different ways we could be intelligent. Although we may have different ways that we process information, how would you rate yourself 0–10 for each of these ways of being intelligent? How would you rate someone you know and someone famous?

Type of intelligence	Me	Someone I know	Someone famous
Linguistic			
Logical-analytical			
Spatial			
Musical			
Naturalist			
Bodily-kinaesthetic			
Interpersonal			
Intrapersonal			

If you are a logical thinker you may also be extremely creative and have a range of different interests. Not all logical thinkers like the same sort of thing or have similar personalities; like we said before, we are complex. It's up to you to think about who you are and how you make sense of the world.

So, if you've decided you process information and experience the world in a more logical way than most, the first thing is to acknowledge that this is valuable and important for both what you would like from your life, and also the world as a whole.

There are many extremely successful people who systematically process information. Historically, there have been many people who have contributed important ideas, invented useful tools and created outstanding systems.

Being a logical systemizer can be excellent.

It can also mean that you may try to look for, interpret and apply systems to social situations. Social communication and interaction cannot always be understood through the application of logic.

People can be complex and our feelings, experiences and behaviour are not always as predictable as we might like. This makes people interesting, and it can also make communication and interaction difficult.

Ben: an example

Over the years I have known lots of logical thinkers. Some have had a high level of *'Naturalist Intelligence'* whilst others have been extremely talented musically or artistically. Some I have met in person and others I have not met, but I know of.

This is Ben:

(This is not actually Ben, this is obviously a graphical representation of him. Look out for more 'untruths' throughout this book!)

Ben was 10 when I first met him.

He was extremely good at mathematical puzzles and could work them out without thinking for very long. This often meant he became bored quickly if he finished these tasks and he also had no interest in spending any time on tasks he felt were unimportant.

Ben is a logical thinker and he would often get frustrated if people misunderstood what he meant, or if he got told off for things he felt made perfect sense.

Ben and I chatted and worked through things. As he was more towards the systematic end of the thinking scale and I was closer to the empathic end, we learned from each other. Ben also scored highly on the *'Logical-Analytical Intelligence Scale'*.

Ben learned from me about himself and why other people behaved in apparently strange ways and from him I learned about coding, 'Terraria' and the details of 'World of Warcraft®'.

Ben also had Asperger's Syndrome. Some people mistakenly assumed things about him.

For example, they thought he could not interpret their facial expressions, and non-verbal communication. This was not the case. Ben realized they were cross or frustrated with him by analyzing their facial expressions and body language.

When Ben was 15 he had an opportunity to tell others about himself. Ben summed it up:

'It's not that I don't realise I've annoyed you, it's just that I don't know *how* I've annoyed you. I need you to tell me so I can avoid doing it again.'

Ben was able to work out how he processed information, what made him annoyed and how he annoyed other people. He also learned that communicating this to others in a particular way meant that they had a better understanding of him too.

Working alongside someone with different skills and a different way of looking at the world helped Ben.

Ben had SOCIAL INTERPRETERS who could advise.

Social Interpreters

Who is in your life that is less logical and more empathic; more able to understand others' behaviour and feelings? There may be people at your home, school, university or place of work that you can think of.

These are your team members. If you know them well and they are happy to help you learn more about this way of thinking, they can become your **'Social Interpreters'** and you may be able to offer them insight into the logical way of thinking. Check with them first and explain that you would like them to be part of your team.

Social Interpreters can help you make sense of why people behave in the way they do and give you ideas on how you can change the way you communicate to non-logical thinkers. This may help improve your experience of working alongside others and help you feel more comfortable being in particular places.

Who are your potential Social Interpreters?

1. ....

2. ....

3. ....

4. ....

The following chapters may help you and your Social Interpreters work through some of the more complex areas of social language and social etiquette.

Notes and ideas

....

....

....

....

....

....

....

....

....

....

....

....

....

....

....

....

....

LANGUAGE
AND
COMMUNICATION

Understanding others

Some people say things that don't make sense at all.

In fact, some spoken and written language can be extremely confusing.

Many words having more than one meaning.

Let us club together to buy a present.

Which golf club would you use to putt?

Are you going to go to the art club after school?

The spoken word can also change meaning through non-verbal aspects of communication such as tone of voice, facial expressions and other body language.

Social language can be different to more technical language. This chapter looks at social language, highlighting some examples and offering explanations for some of those more confusing times.

This is just the start though; you will need your Social Interpreters to help you continue to make sense of what you hear (and see). The tables and diagrams below can be used on these occasions.

People don't make sense!!

Many people use figurative language when speaking.

These are words or phrases that do not necessarily make sense literally but are used to describe something or add interesting elements to conversation.

Idioms, metaphors and similes are types of figurative language. They are a way of speaking which is used to represent something else and means something to those that understand them.

Many people use idioms and metaphors regularly.

Different cultures, countries and geographical areas will use different idioms and metaphors.

If someone says something which does not appear to make sense, they may be using figurative language.

Here are a few to get you started on your exploration of social language. You may have heard them already and know what they mean. Use the thought bubbles to draw out what the phrase would mean if taken literally.

Take a seat

What they really mean: 'Sit down'

Put a sock in it

What they really mean: 'Be quiet'

22

> Go and wash
> your hands in
> the toilet

What they really mean: 'Wash your hands in the sink which is near the toilet area.'

> Who are you most
> comfortable with?

What they really mean: 'Which person are you OK talking to about how you feel?'

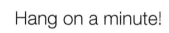

> Hang on a minute!

What they really mean: 'You'll have to wait until I've finished what I am doing or thinking about and then I can listen to what you are saying. This may actually be more or less than a minute.'

23

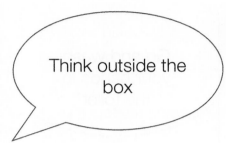

Think outside the box

What they really mean: 'Think about things in a more creative, unconventional way.'

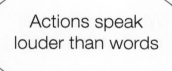

Actions speak louder than words

What they really mean: 'Someone's intentions can be seen in how they behave better than in what they say.'

People don't make sense!!

Record things people say and check-in with a Social Interpreter.

Sometimes thinking about the context you are in as well as what is being said and who is saying it may help add meaning to their words.

There is a table for you to record some of the less logical things you hear and can be used with your Social Interpreter to start deciphering the social comments!

What is said	Where it is said	Who said it	What do they really mean?
E.g. You're on fire today	The classroom	The teacher	You are doing really well.

Sarcasm

Sometimes people can change the meaning of words and phrases by being sarcastic.

Sarcasm is used as a way to mock someone else or make them feel silly. Some people see it as a way to be funny.

Often the speaker's tone of voice will change slightly when they are being sarcastic but sometimes it is difficult to tell if they are being sarcastic unless you know the person well and have learned about how they communicate.

If someone uses sarcasm, it doesn't necessarily mean they are intending to upset you or confuse you, but it may be useful for them to know if you are unsure of what they really mean.

Often when someone is being sarcastic, they actually mean the opposite of what they say.

For example:

You've worked hard on that assignment!

I'm really glad you put your muddy shoes all over my carpet!

Use the following spaces to record some of the occasions you felt someone was being sarcastic. Check-in with your Social Interpreters – do they agree?

Just not true

Why do people often say things that really aren't the truth? We get told to tell the truth, don't we? So, what is it with all of the lies?

Actually, they're not necessarily 'lies'. They may be more theoretical, rhetorical, metaphorical or figurative ways of speaking.

There may also be statements that we say because they are 'politically correct', polite to use or diplomatic.

What they say:

'There's no swearing in school'

Ever heard someone swear in school? Yep? On the playground? At the bus stop? Is the comment above factually correct? No?

What they really mean:

If you swear in front of an adult in school you are likely to be told off.

What they say:

'You should be nice to people'

If this is a rule all people are required to follow, then everyone would be nice to everyone else. Are people always nice to you? Do you feel everyone you know deserves you being nice to them? Is it clear what 'nice' means? No?

What they really mean:

It is socially inappropriate to say things that could be perceived as unkind directly to other people, whether you like them or not. If you do say things they perceive to be unkind, they may avoid you, say something inappropriate back, be physically aggressive towards you or tell others that you are not nice.

What they say:

'You're not listening to me'

Do you hear this from others in the classroom, at home or in other social situations? Are you hearing what they say? Do they insist you are not listening?

What they really mean:

You are not displaying the socially accepted non-verbal cues that you are listening. In most cases this would be

1. Looking towards the speaker

2. Occasionally nodding your head to acknowledge understanding of their words.

3. Responding with a sentence or questions which relates to what they have said and they feel is appropriate.

What they say:

'Your new haircut looks lovely'

Do you hear people commenting on someone else's appearance and you do not agree with their comment? Do they give compliments when you feel they are not true?

There may be more than one reason for this.

1. They have a different opinion to you and they do actually think the other person's haircut looks lovely.

2. They are saying something nice to the person because they like them and want them to feel good.

3. They are being sarcastic and don't really mean it.

What they say:

'I am fine'

When asked 'How are you?' they reply 'I am fine', even if they do not appear to be fine.

In some contexts, it is expected that we won't 'moan' to others and we say we are fine, even if we are not.

What they really mean:

1. I am actually fine.

2. I am not fine but I don't want to talk about it now.

3. I am not fine but I do not want to admit it. I still expect you to try to sort the problem or help me feel better.

What they say:

'If I don't get this finished my teacher will kill me!'

Sometimes we can add emphasis to something we say by adding a more dramatic statement.

This does not mean their teacher really will kill them if they do not complete the assignment.

What they really mean:

I'll be in a lot of trouble if I do not finish my work and hand it in on time.

Record some more confusing or nonsense statements that you hear:

....

....

....

....

....

....

....

What they say:

' '

What they really mean:

What they say:

' '

What they really mean:

What they say:

' '

What they really mean:

What they say:

' '

What they really mean:

Making yourself understood

Do you find you talk to people and they don't seem to understand what you're saying? Or do people seem to often misunderstand you? They may be offended by something and you really did not intend to offend.

Remember, people are good at different things, they have different interests and they process information differently. It may be that adapting the *way* you say something could help reduce misunderstandings.

This section looks at how to adapt the way you speak to increase the chance that others will understand what you mean and your intentions behind what you say.

Do people stop listening to you or walk away when you are telling them about your interests? Do you find they don't always seem interested in what you want to tell them?

This section also helps you think about things you can say and do when you are in a conversation to make sure it is fair and interesting for all.

It's not about changing who you are, but adapting language and conversation to be understood by all, regardless of their interests and expertise.

Try some of the following ways to make yourself better understood.

Change the words

People have different interests and skills and they may have a lot of knowledge on a particular subject.

Some interests come along with their own 'language'.

Take for example 'Lego®'. Often the circles on top are referred to as 'studs' and there are a number of different styles of kits, such as Ninjago, City Lego® and Friends Lego®.

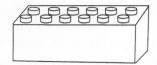

You may understand these terms but if someone is not as interested in Lego®, they may not understand what you are talking about if you use the words without explaining their meaning.

If someone said 'circles' instead of 'studs', they could still make themselves understood by others without using the technical term.

Other people may be interested in car engines.

Words that may be used are:

cylinder

camshaft

alternator

conrod

intake manifold

These words may make no sense to someone who is not familiar with the terms and if the listener is not sure what they mean, the speaker can adapt the words or using other terms to help explain their meaning.

Think about what you are interested in.

Can you think of terms or phrases that apply only to that interest or activity?

Think of some alternative words you could use with those that do not have the same knowledge as you.

Ask others to help if you are unsure.

You have a choice whether you explain the meanings to others or change your language so other people can still understand what you mean.

Words/phrases	Alternatives
Example: studs	Circles, 'bobbles', raised discs, 'bobbly bits'

*****Helpful Hint**** There are no 'right' or 'wrong' ways of making yourself understood. Use whatever language is needed (although best to avoid swearing or inappropriate terms) to help someone else understand what you mean and reduce the risk of misunderstandings**.

36

It is the responsibility of both the speaker and the listener in a conversation to think about how they communicate. The speaker should check whether their words have been understood and the listener should clarify with the speaker to make sure they have received the correct message.

Helpful phrases for the listener:

Can I just check that this is what you meant.....

Am I right in thinking you meant.......

So, I'm just checking, did you mean......

Helpful phrases for the speaker:

Did you understand what I meant?

Shall I explain that another way?

Do you want me to show you what I mean?

Creating compliments

Sometimes it is good to say things to others to help them feel good and to let them know that we have noticed something about them. These are compliments. Using a compliment shows people that we care how they feel. There is not necessarily any practical reason for doing this but it may be appreciated by your family and friends.

Some ways to create a compliment:

1. Notice something about the person that you think is nice. This may be the colour of their eyes, something they are wearing, their haircut, the way they sing etc.

****Social Warning***** There are some things that people don't want others commenting on, even if you intend to be nice. This is especially true if they have only just met you or they don't know you well. In these situations, avoid commenting on parts of the body that would usually be covered by a swimming costume, any hair other than that on their head, wrinkles, spots and moles etc. If you are not sure, speak with your Social Interpreter first!!**

2.   Let them know you have noticed something about them by telling them. They will not be able to know what you are thinking. Try adding positive words so they know it is a good thing.

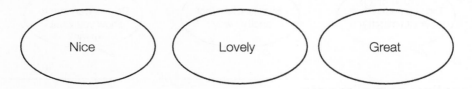

Nice   Lovely   Great

EXAMPLE: That is a nice jacket you are wearing.

3.   Check their response. They may smile or say 'thank you'. They may also tell you something they like about you – returning the compliment. This is good.

Some people find it difficult to accept a compliment and may say 'No it's not!' or disagree with you. Do not be put off, this is often the automatic reaction from some people. They may still be pleased.

Or, they may not put the same value on the focus of the compliment. For example, if you compliment their jacket but they see a jacket simply as an item of clothing, they may not understand the point of the compliment. They may find it more pleasing if the compliment related to their knowledge of a subject.

This may be difficult but it is essential to understand how to give someone a compliment if you would like to help someone feel good. Thinking about how someone is feeling is an important aspect of all kinds of relationships.

It is worth thinking about someone you would like to give a compliment to and discuss the details with your Social Interpreter.

It is the way that you say it!

We may say things that make sense or are factual but the tone we use gives the listener information too.

Have you noticed different people using different tones of voice?

Some ways may make the speaker sound cross or grumpy and others give the impression we are pleased with something.

Another way could make it sound like the speaker is being sarcastic and did not mean what they said.

Have a go:

Step 1

Say: 'The weather seems to have changed today.'

Step 2

Say the same words with a different tone of voice to give the listener the impression you are not happy about the change of weather.

Step 3

Say the same words, this time giving the impression you are happy that the weather has changed. How is your voice different? Is it higher or lower?

Step 4

Say the same words with a sarcastic tone of voice. Practise with a Social Interpreter if needed.

Step 5

Say the same words as if you are very excited by the change in the weather.

Step 6

Repeat Steps 1–5 in front of a mirror (when you are alone) and see if your facial expressions change at all. What happens?

Step 7

Try using different tones for different sentences. You may want to talk about something you are interested in or try saying a compliment with a happy tone of voice.

Step 8

Use different tones of voice with family members or people in school you know well. Get some feedback on how this changes how they perceive what you say.

Social lies

Do you find people don't always tell the truth but others seem to be OK with it? Do you find that when you are honest you can get in trouble for it or people get offended by it?

What you might be experiencing is the result of Socially Acceptable Communication (SAC) vs Factually Accurate Communication (FAC)

Socially acceptable communication – Things that we say that are socially appropriate. These might be things that aren't factually true, that may not be what we actually think or might be just some of what we are thinking. They may also be whole conversation topics that appear to be uninteresting and pointless (sometimes known as 'small talk').

This type of communication also covers 'banter', where people may say things that appear unkind or rude to people they know well.

Factually accurate communication – Anything that is factually correct. These statements may appear rude to others, even if not intended to be.

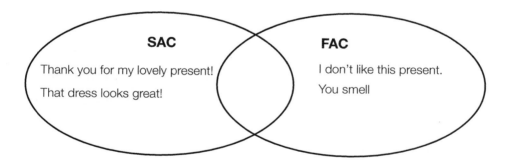

Use this template to place some of the phrases you or others use in social contexts. Think about the ones that don't make sense to you – do they make sense from a social perspective?

Finding the middle way

You may find you are not comfortable with saying things which are socially appropriate, yet factually incorrect.

This is fine. Some logical people I know tell me it feels like a lie if they do this.

Tricky situation then? Don't want to 'lie' but don't want to upset someone?

Try finding the socially acceptable facts!

So, the middle section of the diagram is for phrases that are socially acceptable, yet still factual. **S**ocially **A**cceptable **F**acts

Some examples:

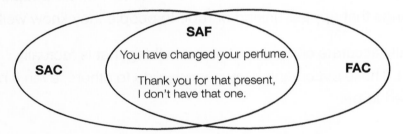

> ********Social Warning******** **Sometimes, when people know each other well, they may use 'banter' to communicate as friends. So, you may hear some people saying things to each other which would not be socially acceptable to say to people you do not have a close relationship with. Look at the next section for more information on this.**

So, it is OK for you to notice things and have an opinion on whether you like something or not.

What you decide to say to someone may be different to what you are thinking.

This is because you may want to avoid hurting their feelings and you may want others around you to feel comfortable being with you.

What I am thinking:

What I could say:

Your new haircut looks awful

Your hair looks different today

Conversations

Having a conversation with someone can be tricky. They may want to talk about things that you are not interested in, or it may be difficult to know when you should speak and when you should listen.

There are different types of talk, different techniques used in conversation and different topics we might discuss with different people!

Confused? You are not the only one!

Try some of the following activities to get you thinking about conversations and then take time to practise with your Social Interpreters.

Topics of conversation

Not everyone is interested in the same thing. You will find you know some people who want to talk about the same things as you. Others have other topics they would like to discuss.

Write down the topics you are interested in:

....

....

....

On a scale of 0–10, how interested are you in each topic?

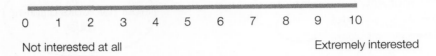

0   1   2   3   4   5   6   7   8   9   10

Not interested at all   Extremely interested

Ask some of the people you know how interested they are in these topics. They may be less or more interested in these topics.

Ask them what things they are interested in. On a scale of 0–10, how interested are you in these things?

When we have conversations with people, it is good to spend some time talking about the things each person is interested in.

This can sometimes feel boring if it is not something that interests you.

The other person may feel bored listening to your interests.

If you would like to be friendly with people who have different interests to you, it is important to sometimes listen to what they would like to talk about.

People are more likely to listen to you if you spend some time listening to them.

To make conversations 'fair', everyone in the conversation should have the opportunity to speak about something. When you speak with someone, give them the opportunity to talk about their interests too.

Try this conversation flowchart:

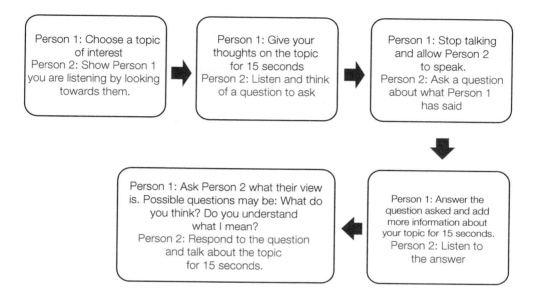

Now repeat the process above, changing roles, so Person 2 starts the conversation with a topic of their choice.

Was it difficult to listen when you wanted to talk? Was it difficult to decide on a topic or stop talking?

This is just one way to have a conversation. Try different time limits, topics of conversation and watch how others talk to each other.

Take some time to create more flowcharts to help structure your conversations.

Pauses

Another important part of a conversation are the pauses. When people pause speaking, they may be giving a message to the listener or listeners that it is their turn to speak if they want to.

It is important that when you have a conversation with someone that you pause every now and then to let them speak. You may want to carry on talking but it is polite to let them speak in the conversation too.

****Social Warning**** Some people pause during their speaking to think about how they want to say something. The ways people talk may be different. If you find out that someone does this, give them a bit more time to continue talking before you speak.

Take some time to watch some people having a conversation. It may be a good idea to watch two people on television doing this first. Some people around you may not be happy with you watching their conversations if you do not know them well or they are not sure what you are doing.

Look out for when there are pauses in the conversation.

How long does each person speak?

Would you say it was a 'fair' conversation?

Try out different length pauses with your Social Interpreter during conversations. Examine what works.

Look like you're listening

When we have a conversation with someone there is usually a time that we would speak and a time that we would listen.

We listen with our ears, and because the words can't be seen, as a listener we have to make it clear that we are have attended to and understood what the speaker is saying.

This means that many people expect us to show we are listening using non-verbal communication. Without speaking, we can use body language and facial expressions to let the speaker know we have heard them.

So, when someone accuses you of 'not listening', what they usually mean is that they would like you to *show* them that you are listening.

Examples of 'good listening' cues are:

1. Glancing towards the speaker.

    This does not mean that you have to stare at the speaker continuously or that you have to make eye contact with them frequently. Try looking towards them every 10 seconds. If you can make eye contact, great but do not worry if not. Just looking towards their face will let them know you are hearing them.

2. Nodding, smiling and frowning

    If we nod every now and then, it gives the speaker the message that we have heard and understood what they are saying. Smiling usually suggests that we feel pleased with what they are saying, or agree with them. If we frown, it would suggest we have heard what they are saying but either do not understand, do not agree with them or we are showing we are concerned about the things they are being said.

3. Face towards the speaker

Although you may be more than capable of listening to someone with your back to them, it is usually expected that, if possible, you turn to face the person talking. This means sitting or standing with the front of your body facing towards the speaker, or just your head and shoulders if your seat is facing in the opposite direction.

4. Fiddle or not?

This is a tricky one and usually comes down to the speaker's preference but sometimes people will expect you to stop what you are doing with your hands and focus just on them. This is not always the case though and many people will be OK with you continuing to do some tasks whilst listening to them. They may expect you to let them know you are listening either by saying:

I am still listening

or by nodding or glancing at them every now and then.

DIFFERENT TYPES OF RELATIONSHIP

=

DIFFERENT TYPES OF COMMUNICATION

We have different people in our lives. Some people are our family and we are related to them. Other people may be our friends and others may be acquaintances. Acquaintances are people we may have met but do not know well.

****Social Warning**** The word 'friends' can relate to different relationships:

1. Social media friends are those online who you communicate with only through technology.

2. Real life friends are those you have met and may see at an educational establishment or in other social situations.

Write down the names of the different people in your life under the different headings.

Family	Social media friends (including online gaming)	Real life friends	Acquaintances

Pick a colour!

Put a tick of this colour next to the names of the people in your table above who you feel understand you the most. Who does not usually get upset or offended when you are honest with them? Who knows you do not intend to hurt them? These people are:

'Close friends'

(this does not mean close geographically or physically)

Pick another colour!

Use this colour to underline the people in your life who you have just met you or have known you for some time but you feel do not understand your way of thinking. Who do you often upset without meaning to?

With the people ticked in the first colour, your 'close friends', you can usually say what you are thinking. You are likely to be able to tell them things that are important to you and personal things about how you feel.

The people in the second group may misunderstand your intentions if you just say what you are thinking. You may want to be more careful about the things you say to them.

Here is a list of topics you may want to talk about.

School or college work	Interests	Relationships
Concerns about being bullied	The weather	Information about weekend plans

Other topics:

There are different reasons we may want to be careful about what we say to particular people.

1. Keeping ourselves safe

There may be lots of good people around you who do not intend to hurt or upset you.

There may also be people around you who do intend to hurt or upset you.

It is sometimes difficult to know what someone is intending to do with the information you give them.

If we give personal information or information that we feel is sensitive about ourselves to people with not good intentions, it may be used to hurt or upset us.

It is not necessarily important to have lots of friends we tell all of our information to. It is more likely that people will choose one or two friends or family members to discuss personal things with and then chat about other topics with more people.

Look at your list again and speak to your Social Interpreters.

Which topics would you talk to your close friends about?

....

....

....

....

Which topics would you discuss with other friends and family members?

....

....

....

....

Which topics would you discuss with acquaintances or people you have just met?

....

....

....

....

*****Social Warning***** You may have had lessons or advice on e-safety. This is about making sure you do not share personal information with people you have just met online through games, forums or other sites. It is also about being careful what you say to others online and remembering that all forms of communication should be thought out. This is to keep you and others safe too. If you are not sure about e-safety, ask your Social Interpreters or research it.

2.   Presenting ourselves

When we say and do things, it gives the people around us a message about who we are. It is the *impression* we give others about ourselves.

If we say things that others find kind or caring, others will see us as a kind and caring person.

If we do or say things that upset someone, even if we do not intend to, others around us may see us as unkind.

People who know us well or understand why we behave the way we do may be OK with you using **F**actually **A**ccurate **C**ommunication. These people understand our *intentions* behind what we say and do. They may understand that we are not meaning to be unkind.

> An **intention** is what we hope from the outcome of our words or actions. So, if I *intend* to upset someone, I can purposefully call them a name I know they would be upset by. If I want to help someone feel good, I can purposefully give them a compliment or buy them a present.

Other people, who we have only just met or who we have known for some time but do not understand the way we are and how we behave may be offended or laugh at us if we were to say the same things to them.

If you find this is happening to you or people avoid you and you are not sure why, it may be that they have misunderstood the intentions behind what you say.

Banter

If you see people who are friends and they seem to be being rude to each other, but OK with it, it may be that they understand that what is being said is a joke and not serious. This type of talk is sometimes known as 'banter' or 'teasing'. It means that both people involved understand that no offense is intended and they are having fun.

Often people may 'tease' each other to show they care. They may feel that they know each other well enough that the other person understands that what they are saying is not true.

Some of your friends and family may appreciate a bit of banter with you.

> *******Social Warning******* **It is only banter if both people are OK. If one person is becoming upset by what is being said and not finding it amusing, it has stopped being banter and it should stop.**

If you are not happy with the banter, it is important to let the other person know. Try saying these things:

If someone knows that you are not happy and they care about how you feel, they will try to stop teasing you.

If they continue to tease and you are not finding it funny, it is important you tell your Social Interpreters or someone who can help.

It is not banter and it could become bullying.

If you are teasing someone as a joke, it is important to make sure they are finding it funny and they are OK with it.

The tricky thing is that sometimes people laugh or smile when they are nervous, not just when they find something funny.

Try saying these things to check in with them:

I'm just checking –
you are OK with me
teasing you like this?

Do let me know if I go
too far with my
teasing – I don't want
to upset you.

If I'm getting too
annoying, tell me to
stop!

If you continue to tease them when they have asked you to stop,
they may become upset and feel like you are bullying them, even if
you have not intended to.

Different types of talk

Small talk

Knowledge talk

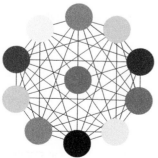

People and feelings talk

Ideas and beliefs talk

1.   Small talk

Firstly, I do not mean 'small talk' in a literal sense.

Small talk is chat with another person or people about topics that don't necessarily educate or inform; topics such as comments on the weather, or questions about what someone plans to do at the weekend.

Although the topics of conversation may appear mundane or unimportant, 'small talk' plays an important role in connecting people socially – engaging in these conversations is like an ice-breaker.

They are a way of acknowledging you are in the presence of another human being and that you care enough to make an effort to engage in conversation.

They are a social tool to enable you to connect on a more superficial level before discussing more complex topics. In most social situations the expectation would be to start with 'small talk' before speaking at length on your topic of interest.

What other things do people talk about that fit into this type of conversation?

Listen to others around you and complete the table below with your observations. Keep a record and see if there are any patterns with people or places?

	Small talk
What was being discussed?	
Who was there?	
Where were they?	
Were you interested?	

2. Knowledge talk

Many people like to talk about things that are factual. They may want to share knowledge of interests or information they have learned recently. These may be things they have discussed in academic lessons or they may have read about or seen on the internet or television.

You may find people who share similar interests will spend more time speaking with each other on their interest. Or it may be that those that have different interests but prefer talking about factual information are more likely to converse in this way more often.

You may hear these types of conversations in particular places, or when you are around particular people who prefer to engage in discussions around facts.

Listen to others and record your observations on this type of talk.

	Knowledge talk
What was being discussed?	
Who was there?	
Where were they?	
Were you interested?	

3.   People and feelings talk

Many people prefer to talk about people and feelings.

They may talk about themselves and their interactions with others and how they felt about experiences.

They may be comfortable crying in front of others or comforting others when they cry or shout.

This kind of talk involves discussing what we have seen or heard others do or say. Some of the things we talk about may not involve real people – it may be conversations about television programmes such as Soap Operas (or 'soaps', but not the type used to clean yourself) and what the characters may be experiencing.

There may be certain places you are more likely to hear this type of talk. Listen to others and record your observations.

	People and feelings talk
What was being discussed?	
Who was there?	
Where were they?	
Were you interested?	

4.   Ideas and beliefs talk

Talking about ideas involves discussing thoughts we have had on things and developing them into original ideas.

Because people are interested in different things, these ideas may involve different topics. For example, they may be ideas on coding or horticulture or architecture. Any topics can be included in this category.

It is more than just the information on an area, ideas talk is about how to take ideas further. It is the creation of new ideas or examining problem solving around issues or experiences.

They may also involve ideas on how to achieve particular levels or navigate quests on games.

Ideas and beliefs talk could also include our opinions on events, experiences and topics.

	Ideas and beliefs talk
What was being discussed?	
Who was there?	
Where were they?	
Were you interested?	

Think about the different types of conversations we have.

Remember we are different, so may be more or less likely to engage in the different types of conversation.

You may prefer a particular type of conversation and find other types boring or not useful. Others may feel the same about the type of conversation you prefer.

This is OK.

Think about the types of 'talk' and the people around you. Who are you most likely to engage in these conversations with?

Small talk:

....

....

....

Knowledge talk:

....

....

....

People and feelings talk:

....

....

....

Ideas talk:

....

....

....

One conversation may include more than one type of talk.

Here is an example:

'Hi, how are you?'

'Good thanks, did you have a good weekend?'

'Yes thanks, I played on the new game that has just come out'

'Ok, what did you think of it?'

'It was good, but a bit too easy really.

'Why?'

'It only took me a few hours to complete the first three levels. If I was them I would have included harder quests in level 2 and not allowed unlocking of all of the characters until they'd been completed.'

Can you identify the different types of talk in this conversation?

It may be that you decide to try out different types of 'talk' to help you connect with others. (Not literally! I told you language was strange!)

Make it visual!

Communicating with others can be difficult.

Sometimes we cannot seem to find the words we would like to use and sometimes we say things that unintentionally upset or annoy others.

If we are experiencing strong feelings ourselves, it may be that we find it more difficult to present ourselves in the way we would like and we may become annoyed that we haven't expressed ourselves in the way we intended.

It is important to remember there is more than one way to communicate.

If you can't find the right words to say, try drawing or writing them down!

Sometimes if we are trying to explain a solution to a problem or give someone information, it can be presented more effectively in a diagram or table.

Here is an example.

Communication tools:

Verbal	Non-verbal
• Spoken in person • Skype • Telephone • Webcam	• Texts • Typed notes or messages • Email • Body language • Facial expressions • Signing • Drawn diagrams • Drawn cartoon strips • Tables • Graphs • Written equations

Add more communication tools to the diagram.

Different communication tools can be useful at different times.

Have you ever wanted to tell someone about an experience you have had? Have you found it hard to put the events in the correct order and be clear what happened when telling them verbally?

Draw it!

An effective alternative way to communicate is by drawing it out.

Start with:

- Where you were
- Who was there
- What you were doing

Now think about what happened:

Include what people said:

What you were thinking:

What you were feeling:

Try to remember details and add as many pictures as you need until you feel you have communicated what you need.

Build it!

Other ways to communicate might include using plasticine or building blocks (like Lego®) to create a representation of your ideas or thoughts.

Here's an example.

What if you find a particular lesson difficult but you're not sure how to explain why.

Step 1

Build a mini version of the classroom using Lego® bricks.

Step 2

Use a brick or Lego® person to represent you in the classroom.

Step 3

Move the brick or person to explain:

- Where you usually sit

- Where you feel most happy in the classroom

- Where you feel the least happy in the classroom

Step 4

Use other bricks or Lego® people to represent other people in your class.

Step 5

Move the bricks or people to explain:

- Who sits near you

- Where the teacher or support staff are

- Who you most like to be near

- Who you least like to be near

Step 6

Use the model of the classroom to show where you find it the most noisy and give information about different smells and sounds you experience in different parts of the classroom.

Notes and ideas

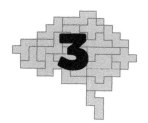

3

SOCIAL
BEHAVIOUR

Logically correct
or socially
appropriate?

Sometimes the way people behave does not always appear to make sense.

You may have noticed you are expected to do things which you do not see any point in, such as queueing or holding doors open for others. These are examples of social etiquette; the way others expect us to behave. These types of behaviour may be different in different in different places, countries, schools or even different families. The way others expect us to behave changes depending on the context we are in and the relationship with have with the people around us.

Complicated isn't it?!

Understanding social etiquette and being able to work out how we should behave in different places can be confusing and tiring. Very few people get it 'right' immediately and most people still make mistakes at times.

Ask your Social Interpreters if they have ever hugged someone who they realized afterwards did not want a hug? If they think and process information on social etiquette well and they still make mistakes, it shows how tricky it is!

This chapter offers guidelines on some areas of social interaction. Some of the rules are not always clear and things do change, so, try not to get too frustrated with yourself if you find it doesn't work out how you would like all of the time!

Keep trying and keep working with your team!

Rule breaking: managing the illogical

Do others break the rules and get away with it?

How about when the rule is to stay in line and you have been standing there, sticking to the rule then you see someone in front of you let their friend join them? That doesn't seem fair or right, yet no-one seems to mind. Why is that?

ME   Rule breaker

Or the rule on the sign that you should always walk on the left down corridors, and yet you see people walking on the right.

Strange?

Unfair?

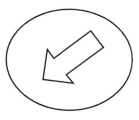

KEEP LEFT

What about when you are playing a game with someone: Sports? Board game? Multi-player console game?

Do you feel like you have a clear understanding of the rules and then someone breaks them or changes them?

Why are others not upset by this?

Social rules do not always fit neatly into 'right' or 'wrong' and some rules can be changed or adapted depending on the situation. This does not always seem right to a logical thinker who likes to stick to the rules and for the rules to stay the same for everyone.

RIGHT   SOCIAL RULES   WRONG

This is what people mean when they say:

Things are not always black and white!

Let's look at some rules that do not always stay the same.

Younger people – different rules

We all take time to learn rules and sometimes we need more time to learn them.

It may seem that those younger than you are 'getting away' with not sticking to the rules but it might be that they are still practising and need more time.

It may be that you are expected to behave differently because you are older or you may be expected to show the younger children how they should be behaving.

You are more likely to get into trouble if you break the rules than a younger person as you have had more time to learn what you should be doing.

This can feel frustrating and unfair. It is something you may have to manage.

As the younger person gets older, they will probably be expected to understand more and are likely to have the same consequences as you if they do not stick to the rules.

Ignoring or disobeying signs

There are many signs displaying rules:

Often you may see people ignore the rules. If you are someone who always sticks to the rules, this can be very annoying.

The person ignoring the sign:

1. May not have seen it

2. May have seen it but have permission to ignore it

3. May have seen it and decided they are going ignore it and risk getting the consequence

It is important that everyone is allowed to choose how they behave. You do not have to behave in the same way if you do not want to.

If someone else breaks the rules and ignores the signs, they risk getting a consequence.

For example, if a teacher sees them walking the wrong side of the corridor, they may get told off.

If you feel you want to tell someone about these rules being broken you could:

A. Choose to tell the person directly or

B. Decide not to approach the rule-breaker but check with your Social Interpreter first.

If you choose A, be aware that not everyone likes being reminded they are breaking a rule. Even though you may be right, they may get annoyed that you are telling them. You'd think they'd be happy you were helping them right?

Sometimes, but not always!

They may be more likely to be annoyed if they fit into the No. 3 category and they are aware of the rule breaking.

If you choose B, you can discuss with your Social Interpreter who will talk to you about whether it is important to tell someone else about it.

If you still feel strongly that you should tell them directly, that is up to you.

Perception

People see things differently.

Have a look at the picture.

What do you see?

Some people see two faces and others see a vase or candlestick. Some people can see both.

The picture has not changed, but how we see it may be different.

This can be true for other experiences and situations.

How we see or understand things is about perception. My perception of a situation may be different to yours.

If we take time to try to understand someone else's perception of a situation it may reduce misunderstandings.

Misunderstandings can cause arguments. Reducing misunderstandings may also reduce arguments with people we care about.

If we can be clear about how we view things and communicate effectively, we can make sure other people have a better understanding of what we think and feel. They may still have different views and ideas but they may be able to understand our point of view better.

Here is a scenario:

Fred wants to borrow some games from Aisha.

Two weeks later, Aisha wants her games back and is cross that Fred has not returned them.

Who is right? They have their own points of view on the situation.

Other expectations can cause problems.

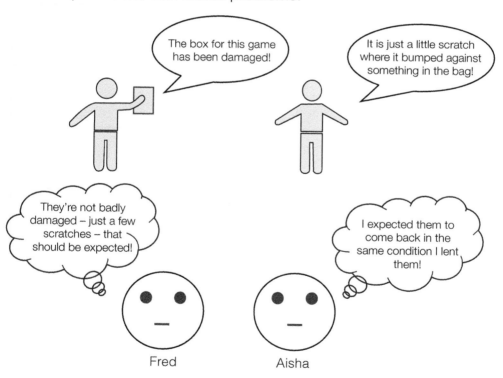

People may have different points of view, different expectations and different ideas. One way to help reduce issues later is to be clear with your thoughts on things.

It might help to write up expectations before lending someone something.

Have a look at the following template. It could be used in a sharing/ swapping situation to clarify thoughts before agreeing to the swap.

Trading rules
Discuss and agree terms beforehand to reduce the risk of misunderstandings.
Item/s
Length of time of trade:
Expected condition on return:
Other terms:

By communicating your thoughts clearly, you help the other person understand your views and expectations and reduce the risk of misunderstandings.

Draw out or write down a scenario where there has been a misunderstanding due to perception.

Remember to record things all people said and did if you can.

Can you see how they see things? Can you understand their point of view, even though you may not agree with it?

How offensive?!

Have you ever been upset by someone and when you have tried to stand up for yourself you have ended up getting in more trouble?

Do you find it strange that some words or behaviour seems to be ok but others can get you in serious trouble?

Like a lot of things in the social world, there is not necessarily a 'right' or 'wrong' but it can be seen as more of a scale. Many words and actions can be placed on this scale from 'mildly irritating' to 'extremely offensive or inappropriate':

The scale of offensiveness/ inappropriateness

Mildly irritating

Extremely offensive/ inappropriate

*****Warning****** There is a list of words below some may find offensive. No offence is intended but you may prefer not to complete the activity if you feel uncomfortable using the words.**

Look at the words and actions below. Place them on the scale of how offensive you find them.

WORDS:

Bloody	Fuck	Idiot	Twat	Bugger
Cunt	Spastic	Knobhead	Cock	Dickhead
Bitch	Arse	Wanker	Bollocks	Shit

Add more that you hear...

....

....

Actions:

Spitting on the ground

Laughing (at someone who has fallen over

Not holding the door open for someone coming through behind you

Hitting someone

Kicking someone

Throwing litter on the ground

Making the swearing
sign at someone

Pointing and laughing
at someone's spots

Riding your bike on
the pavement

Add other actions that you or someone you know may find
inappropriate or offensive:

....

....

....

Which words and actions do you find the least offensive?

....

....

Which do you think would be the most inappropriate to use at
school or work?

....

....

Other people may think differently. Some people may find all of
these things inappropriate and others may not be offended at all by
any of them.

Find out from your Social Interpreters where they would place words
and actions on the scale.

Context

It is important to consider how other people view words and
behaviours. In some places, with people you know, you may hear

many of the words being used and in other places, you may find there would be more serious consequences for using them.

You may find it is ok to laugh at someone who knows you well but not ok to laugh at the same action by someone you have only just met.

****** Social Warning***** Some of the words are illegal to use in public in some countries and you could be in serious trouble if you used them.

Consider these contexts and decide where you may or may not use particular words or actions:

School corridor	Café in town	Public bus	Car with friends
Your room at home	School field/ playground	Alone in a field	At the cinema
In a supermarket	At a football game	Gaming online	Gaming alone

Public social media page

Other places:

....

....

....

....

Consequences

There are often consequences to using particular words or actions. The consequences of using extremely inappropriate or offensive language and behaviour could include things you may be aware of immediately and also reactions that you may not be aware of.

- A verbal or physical retaliation from others

- Punishment at school or home

- Warnings in work situations

- Bans from social events or public places

- Bans from websites, forums or online gaming communities

- Other people deciding not to sit with you during social occasions

Consider whether you are aware of all of the consequences and discuss with your Social Interpreter other things that may happen if you continue to use particular words or act in a certain way.

It is up to you what you decide to do, however it is important to be aware of some of the consequences so you can make an informed choice.

Working in groups

Does it ever feel you are asked to put aside your brilliant ideas, in order to go with what someone else wants?

Doesn't make sense, right? Especially when you're right and your idea is clearly better!

Well, the thing is sometimes we have to work with others and in order for that to be successful, we have to let others have choices that we might not agree with. (See also 'Facts and opinions' section)

Working in groups can be difficult.

Everyone may have different ideas and views. Also, some people will be more confident to say their ideas and others may struggle to manage their emotions if they feel they are not listened to.

It can also be great!

Sometimes we can learn from other people's ideas and when people with different ways of thinking learn how to work well together, the final result could be more valuable or more effective than if one person worked alone.

How well do you work in a group?

Do you insist on your ideas being used? Do you let others speak? Are you worried about saying what you think?

Try the following techniques out with your Social Interpreters:

1. Hearing everyone's ideas

If someone in a group is not listened to, we may miss out on valuable information or important ideas. To make sure everyone is able to say what they think, try these guidelines:

- Have a 'talking object' (an item such as a pen or cup) which is passed around the group. Only the person holding the object is allowed to speak. Each person has the object for an equal amount of time before discussing all of the ideas.

- Have a rule that NO IDEA WILL BE LAUGHED AT. It is sometimes difficult to say what you think if you are worried about how others will react. No matter how strange the idea may sound, others should listen respectfully, even if they do not find it interesting or useful.

NO LAUGHING AT IDEAS

- Use different methods of communication. If someone does not want to speak, can they write, text, draw, sign, build or email their ideas?

Method of communication	√	✗
Speak		
Write (on paper, post-it note, whiteboard etc.)		
Sign		
Text		
Draw		
Build (with Lego® or modelling clay etc.)		
Email		
Other		

2. Speak calmly and assertively

Working in a group may mean we have the opportunity to share our ideas. Some people are confident speaking in front of a group of people, others get worried or do not like it.

If you have an idea, it may be valuable and others may find it useful. Some people may agree with you and others may not.

This is ok. Remember, people think differently and have different views. This is very important in a group.

If you say your ideas calmly and with confidence, you are more likely to get people to listen to you. This is about clearly communicating your idea, clarifying details when others ask questions and explaining how it will fit with the identified task.

Try these things:

- Write or draw your ideas down before you offer them or whilst you are talking to the group.
- Confidently say 'I have an idea!'
- Speak loud enough for everyone in the group to hear.

- Explain your general idea, adding details later.

- Link it to the task you have been given.

- Ask if anyone has any questions.

- Be prepared to adjust some details of your idea if others offer them and they work with your idea.

3. Learn to compromise sometimes

Being able to compromise is an important skill when working in a group.

Your ideas may be used sometimes and at other times you may have to let other people's ideas be used or let someone else complete a task you would have preferred to do.

Often in groups it is a majority decision. If most people decide on someone else's idea, it may mean you have to complete the task in a way you do not like. The task may end up successful or it may end up that you think you could have done it better yourself.

Being able to compromise and accept others' ideas can be difficult. It may help to say things like:

I like your idea, but how about we adjust it slightly in this way………

How about we use your idea this time and mine next time?

It's not something I would have thought of, but we can give it a go.

You can also try getting everyone to write their ideas down and pick one from each person, depending on how many you need. Although it may not be all of your ideas used, it will feel fair for everyone.

Name of group member	Idea 1	Idea 2	Idea 3	Chosen idea

Even if your idea is not used, it does not mean it was not a good idea, it just means that the group decided to use a different one.

4. Manage disappointment and frustration

Disappointment and frustration are feelings.

When we do not get to do the things we want, in the way we want, we may feel disappointed.

We may feel frustrated if things do not go the way we planned or hoped for.

This is OK.

Disappointment and frustration can be difficult to manage and they may make us feel like crying or shouting or walking out of the room or hitting someone or throwing something.

If we want to successfully work in a group, it is something we have to try to manage appropriately, but it is completely natural to feel this way.

Managing disappointment and frustration appropriately means learning to behave in a way that does not hurt ourselves or someone else. It also means that if we want to successfully continue to work in a group, we should manage it in a way that others are ok with.

For example:

If your idea was chosen in the group and someone else was disappointed because theirs was not, would you expect them to shout at you, or throw something or not participate in your idea?

How would you feel if they did one of those things? What would you think and would you choose them to be in your group again?

It is OK that they are disappointed but you would expect them to behave in a particular way. How would you expect them to be?

This applies to you too. Others in your group will have an expectation of how people should behave.

If you are disappointed try:

- Telling yourself that it you may get your choice next time.
- Channel your feeling into putting as much effort as possible into the chosen idea, even if you don't agree with it. Others will notice your effort and your group is more likely to succeed at the task, even if it not your first choice of idea.
- Take a few minutes away from the group, e.g. in the toilets or getting a drink if possible, to allow yourself to feel OK again before coming back to continue with the task.

Sometimes tasks can be more difficult than we anticipated or people decide to do things in different ways.

If you are frustrated during a task try:

- Telling your group members that you are finding something frustrating – they may also be feeling this way.
- Stop what you are doing briefly in order to be ok again and then continue.
- Ask someone in your group for help with the task you are doing.
- Attempt to complete another task and come back to the one you are getting frustrated with.
- Take a break for a few minutes, get a drink if possible and return to the task when you are ok.

Think of some other strategies with your Social Interpreters.

-
-
-
-

> ***Social Warning***** There are guidelines as to what strategies you can use to help manage feelings. Try sticking to these guidelines whilst choosing strategies:
>
> 1. **It must not hurt me**
>
> 2. **It must not hurt someone else**
>
> 3. **It must not break or ruin something important**
>
> **These guidelines will keep you and others safe and avoid important things getting broken.**

Motivate

Working in groups is not always easy.

Sometimes learning to help motivate and encourage your team members will lead to a more successful outcome. Also, learning to remain self motivated when there are challenges will be more likely to result in a successful outcome.

Motivate others by saying:

Think of other motivating things to say:

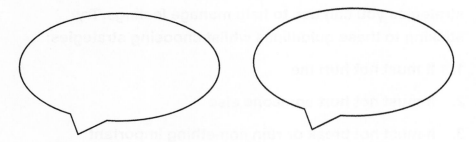

Motivate yourself by thinking:

I can do this…...

I'm feeling frustrated because I care!

The harder the challenge, the more satisfying the success!

Doing my best is good enough.

Think of other motivating things to think:

Celebrate all achievements!

Even if the task is not completed in the way you would like, if the objective of the activity or session has been achieved, it is important to acknowledge this.

Sometimes we may feel individuals in the group could have done better, however if the group has worked well, with problems being solved and feelings managed appropriately, this can be seen as an achievement and should be celebrated!

Team members are more likely to want to work with people who can acknowledge success.

Try these:

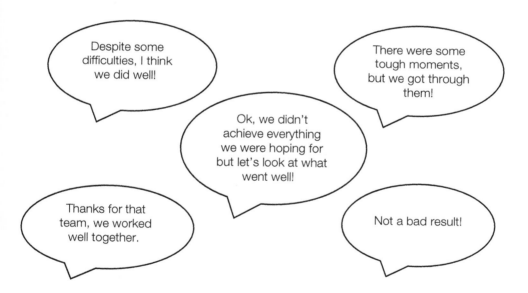

To hug or not to hug?! That is the ultimate question!

This section deals with not just hugging, but different kinds of physical contact and how to consider what is appropriate.

Social touch

Have you ever noticed people touching?

Hugs?

Holding hands?

High fives?

Hitting their friends for fun?!!

There are many ways we show people we care about them through touch.

It can get confusing who it is OK to touch and when.

Have you ever gone to hug someone and then got told not to? Or have you been hugged by someone when you really didn't want a hug?

There are many things to take into consideration when you think about whether it is appropriate to give someone a hug or any form of touch. When I asked a group of teachers about this, they found it hard to work out the rules!

There are some strict laws about some forms of touching that it is important to know.

Speak with your Social Interpreter about these laws and how they relate to people of different ages. Record them here:

....

....

....

....

....

As well as different laws about age, the most important thing is that both people must feel OK with it.

Some of us like hugs, some of us don't.

This is OK. Regardless of the rest of this section, if you do not want to hug people, you do not have to.

That's the most important thing to understand here.

So, here are some things to think about and discuss with your Social Interpreter, but be aware this is a complex issue!

Who?

The relationship you have with someone is one of the most appropriate considerations. If you hug someone who you do not have a good relationship with, they may feel extremely uncomfortable.

Think about these people. Who might you hug? (NB. You may not have all of these people in your life; that is OK, just circle the ones which are relevant to you).

Teacher	Mum	Close friend	Someone you sit next to in class
Brother	Bus driver	Shop cashier Sister	Step-Dad
Someone you like but do not talk to very often		Aunt	Neighbour
Step-Mum	Grandmother	Cousin Uncle	Stranger at the bus stop
Support worker in school or college		Girlfriend/ Boyfriend	Grandfather

Work colleague

Other:

Where?

Sometimes people may be ok with hugging but where you are needs to be considered. There are some places it is more appropriate to hug than others. Where would you hug people?

Classroom	Bus	Playground/ Field at school	Shop
Home	Town	Café	Canteen in school/ work

Other:

Why?

There are many reasons why you may give someone a hug, or would like a hug from someone.

To comfort someone who is upset	To share happiness and excitement	To feel better when you are upset
To express affection or love	To greet someone	To say goodbye to someone

Other:

When?

There may be times that it is more appropriate to hug someone. Consider these times and think about when it would be appropriate.

After school/ work   During a lesson   During work   At break/ lunch

Other:

How?

There are different ways to hug someone. How you hug them may make them feel more or less comfortable. Think about these ways:

Quick hug   Long hug   Both arms   One arm over their
                                                          shoulder

Facing them   When they have
                      their back to you

Other:

> ****Social Warning**** If you would like to hug or touch
> someone it is extremely important that they are happy for
> you to do so. You may see other people hugging but this
> does not mean they will be happy for you to touch them too.
>
> There are many elements to the rules around hugging. If
> you are not sure you should check with them first. Hugging
> or touching someone when they do not want you to could
> be inappropriate or illegal.
>
> If you do not want someone to hug or touch you, that is
> OK and you should make sure you are clear that you would
> rather not be hugged.

Not sure? Try saying:

Is it ok if I give you a hug?

If you or someone else does not like hugging, try these alternatives:

High Fives   Handshakes   Tap on arm or shoulder

Other:

....

....

....

Winning and losing

Losing is rubbish.

I don't know anyone who likes losing. You might know someone, but I certainly don't.

Losing, however, is often an expected aspect of taking part in a game, competition or challenge and so it is something we may have to manage.

There are different reasons why we may want to be able to manage losing:

1. To allow us to have a socially acceptable response to losing and therefore be more likely to be asked to take part in activities again.

If we decide to respond to losing by throwing things, shouting or becoming physically aggressive to others, we are less likely to be asked to join in activities again as others will not want to risk a similar reaction.

If we can lose and manage our disappointment and annoyance appropriately, others will see us as someone who they can trust to be ok whilst playing games or taking on challenges.

2. To allow us to keep taking on challenges and so improve our own skills and develop further.

If we decide we do not want to ever experience losing, we are likely to only play games with people we know we can win against or take on tasks which we are confident we can beat everyone else at. This is OK but it means our skills may not improve as we are not being challenged.

If we want to get better at something we may have to risk losing against someone better than us, in order to push ourselves (not literally!) to get better and better.

How to be a 'good loser'

As we have established, losing may not feel great.

It is important to recognise this and to manage our feelings around losing in a way that is socially appropriate.

Take a look at the actions below and circle all of the actions which most people would not find acceptable:

Throwing a chair	Hitting the other team/player	Shaking hands
Spitting at the other team/ player	Walking away	Kicking furniture

Smiling (even when you may not feel like it)

Shouting loudly at others

Other actions:

....

....

....

Although we may feel like doing all of these things, we should try to do only some of them.

Losing well can be very difficult but it is a skill we can learn with practice.

Try saying some of these things if you find you have lost:

Wow, that was a lot harder than I thought it would be.

Never mind, maybe I'll win next time.

Well played, you are a worthy opponent!

That was close, but well done for winning in the end.

I'll definitely beat you next time!

Good game!

Think of other things you can say to help yourself feel better whilst also being socially acceptable:

Winning

Winning can be great.

It can make us feel like jumping up and down or running around!

We might be tempted to shout about it and loudly tell people how great we are and how rubbish they are because we won and they lost:

If we say and do things like this, it might upset the people we want to play games with and they may be less likely to want to play again!

It is good to feel happy we won and we should be able to express that we are happy, however we should also take other people's feelings into consideration.

If they were to win next time - would you be happy if they said the same to you?

Being a 'good winner' is as important as being a 'good loser'.

Try saying these things:

Good game!

I enjoyed that game – you played well!

You only just lost!

Phew, that was a tough one – I had to work hard for that win!

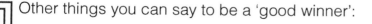

Other things you can say to be a 'good winner':

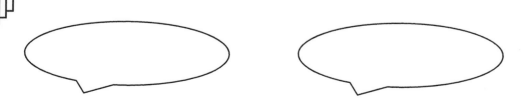

Facts and opinions

Have you ever told someone what you know to be true and they insist you are wrong?

Have you had to write 'two points of view' in school assignments?

What you might be experiencing is Facts vs Opinions.

Although you may feel certain that what you are saying is true, it may be that you have a very strong opinion on something. This does not make it a fact.

People may try to present an opinion as fact. This does not make it a fact. This just means they are persuasive.

Facts are things that are known or proved to be true.

Opinions are beliefs or feelings that someone has on something.

Here are some examples:

FACTS

An apple is a fruit

William Shakespeare was an author

1 + 1 = 2

There are many types of musical instruments

The plural of 'bee' is 'bees'

OPINIONS

Football is rubbish

Cereal can only be eaten at breakfast

William Shakespeare is the best English author

Art galleries are boring

We shouldn't have to wear school uniform

Now decide where these statements go:

Pink is for girls

Wind turbines are the best form of renewable energy

Harry Potter is a character from a book

Paris is the capital of France

Mashed potatoes are better than roast potatoes

Baby seals are called pups

The difference between a 'Fact' and an 'Opinion' is that you can have more than one opinion.

Having a different opinion to someone does not mean that you are wrong and they are right.

It does not mean that you are right and they are wrong.

It simply means you have different ideas.

Thunks®

Someone called Ian Gilbert has written a great (in my opinion) book on 'Thunks®'. It is called *The Little Book of Thunks®: 260 Questions to Make Your Brain Go Ouch!*

'Thunks®' are questions or statements that make you think. They do not have a right or wrong answer but you can use them to discuss your thoughts and argue your viewpoint.

Try some:

'Is it ever right to bully a bully?'

'Should stupid people be allowed to vote?'

'Can a dog be kind?'

'If I tell a joke that is translated who is making the other person laugh – me or the translator?

Gilbert (2007)

Expressing opinions

Sometimes we can be really sure that our opinion is the 'right' way of thinking and we want to make sure everyone knows it.

Other times we may not feel like we want to express our opinion in case others laugh or do not agree with us.

Our opinion matters. Even if it feels like we are the only ones with that opinion, we are allowed to have it and we should feel we can express it.

Other people's opinions matter. Just because they may have a different opinion to us, they should still feel like they can express it.

How we express our opinion is important.

We have a right to express our opinions but we also have a responsibility to make sure we express them in a way that respects other people's opinions.

This can sometimes be hard, especially if both people have strong opinions.

Think about these three ways:

> ## Passive:
> accepting what others say and do without responding

> ## Aggressive:
> being confrontational or forceful and intimidating

> ## Assertive:
> confidently, calmly and clearly expressing ideas

If you remain passive and do not tell people your opinions your ideas may never be heard.

If you are aggressive, your words may be heard but you may never know if others actually agree with you or if they are just scared to say what they think.

If you are assertive, you will be able to voice your opinions with the likelihood that others will feel confident to express theirs.

Learning to be assertive may take time and practise. It is worth trying to express your opinions in this way as people will be more likely to listen to you, understand your viewpoint and engage in more conversations with you.

Try out different ways of expressing your opinions with your Social Interpreters, using some 'Thunks®' as discussion points.

Notes and ideas

....

....

....

....

....

....

....

....

....

....

....

....

....

....

....

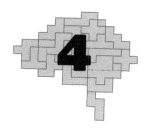

ACTION PLAN

Action plan
Steps to success

This action plan could be used to help improve some skills to make you feel more comfortable and happier being around other people if that's what you want.

It could be used to help you improve the way you get your point across assertively and clearly or it may be that you want to work on improving your group work skills.

It should not be used to try to change your whole personality – you are important as a person as you are and your opinions and beliefs matter.

1. **Decide on your goal** (e.g. Allowing others to speak in conversations)

2. **Draw out your own Goal Marker.** Avoid it looking like neat steps......

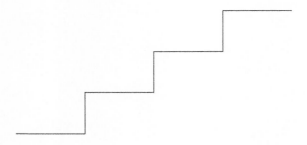

It is more likely to look like this:

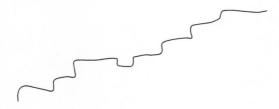

New skills take time to learn and practise so there may be occasions when you feel you are not reaching your goal as quickly as you would like. Perseverance will make it more attainable.

It may change shape as you take steps towards your goal so change the Goal Marker when needed.

3. What skills do I have already?

Think about what you already do well – e.g. 'I am able to start a conversation with my friend'.

Put these skills on some of the lower steps.

4. What are my next steps?

Think about small steps to start to achieve your goal, e.g. 'Speak with my Social Interpreter about how to hide my boredom whilst listening to others' or 'practise listening to topics I am not interested in'.

Put these steps on your Goal Marker and practise.

*****HANDY TIP!****

OBSERVE OTHERS

What do you see others doing in similar situations? (Remember this may not seem logical!)

What they say/ don't say:

Tone and volume of voice:

What they do:

(e.g. looking towards the speaker, waiting for others to speak, nodding etc.)

What was the response from others?

5. **Carry out your small steps.** Think about:

   - When I used it

   - What happened? How did others respond?

6. **Check-in with your Social Interpreter** – what worked? What didn't work? Are you going to adjust anything for the next practice opportunity or do you feel you have mastered the skill? If you feel you have successfully mastered the skill, think about the next steps.

7. **Repeat steps 4–6.**

8. Once you have reached your goal, reflect on the process and your success. **Celebrate.**

Remember learning new skills is something everyone is doing and it can take time. You may feel you have got it right immediately or it may take many attempts to reach your goal.

Persevere.

Action plan

1. Decide on your goal:
2. Draw out your own Goal Marker:
3. What skills do I have already?
4. What are my next steps?

5. Carry out your small steps. What happened? How did others respond?

6. Check in with your Social Interpreter. Make any notes here:

7. Repeat steps 4–6. Note any observations here:

8. Celebrate!

References and further reading

Autism Research Centre (ARC) (n.d.) 'About Professor Simon Baron-Cohen'. Available from: https://www.autismresearch centre.com/people_Baron-Cohen

Baron-Cohen, S. (2004) *The Essential Difference: Men, Women and the Extreme Male Brain*. Penguin Books, London.

Gardner, H. (n.d.) *The Theory of Multiple Intelligences*. Available from: http://multipleintelligencesoasis.org/wp-content/uploads/2013/06/443-davis-christodoulou-seider-mi-article.pdf

Gardner, H. (2011) *Frames of Mind: The Theory of Multiple Intelligences*. Basic Books, New York.

Gardner, H. (2006) *Multiple Intelligences: New Horizons*. Basic Books, New York.

Gardner, H. (2009) *Multiple Intelligences Around the World*. Jossey-Bass, New York.

Gilbert, I. (2007) *The Little Book of Thunks®: 260 Questions to Make Your Brain Go Ouch!*. Crown House Publishing Ltd, Carmarthen, UK.

Smith, M. K. (2002, 2008) 'Howard Gardner and multiple intelligences', *The Encyclopedia of Informal Education*. Available from: http://infed.org/mobi/howard-gardner-multiple-intelligences-and-education/

For Product Safety Concerns and Information please contact our EU
representative GPSR@taylorandfrancis.com Taylor & Francis Verlag GmbH,
Kaufingerstraße 24, 80331 München, Germany

Printed and bound by CPI Group (UK) Ltd, Croydon, CR0 4YY
11/04/2025
01843977-0012